THE LBL MASSACRE

BY

STEVE CAUSEY

SECOND EDITION

THE LBL MASSACRE

BY

STEVE CAUSEY

SECOND EDITION

*"There are more things in Heaven and Earth,
than are dream't of in your Philosophy."*

* From William Shakespeare Hamlet, Act 1, Scene 5

First Edition published 2023

Second Edition published 2024

Foreword

There are places on earth that still exist today, where you can put your hand in front of your face on a moonless night and not be able to see your fingers, the Land Between the Lakes is one of these places. We tend to think because of our technology and many electronic gadgets and cell phone towers that there are few places on earth that we cannot travel and feel at home and comfortable. The Land Between the Lakes is the largest inland peninsula in the United States, there are almost 200,000 square acres of land within this area and almost 300 miles of shoreline. The Land Between the Lakes, also known as the "LBL" is one of the most pristine and beautiful places on earth. The LBL is a hunting, fishing, and camping paradise, unrivaled in the United States, It is also a very desolate place that nature has reclaimed. You can walk for miles in the LBL and never see another person and still have miles to travel before you leave the area. Most of this area has no cell phone towers, and cell phones simply do not work there. There are few repeater towers for law enforcement in this area, so their emergency radios are limited. The only viable means of communications in this area are satellite-based phones and other devices that use this technology. The canopy of the trees in some areas of the LBL has grown to about 90 percent, and even with satellite phones, one might have to find a clearing to communicate.

Chapter 1

Brief History of the Land Between the Lakes

The recorded history of this area goes back to the 1600s when the French were establishing settlements along the Cumberland and Tennessee rivers. Shawnee Indians established settlements along the rivers from Nashville Tennessee to as far north as Kentucky from the late 1600's through the mid-1700s. This area was commonly known as the Land between the Rivers until the 1960s. During the Civil War the Confederates established river forts in this area on both the Tennessee River and the Cumberland River. Fort Henry was the Confederate stronghold on the Tennessee River, however this fort was built on low-lying land and was quickly overwhelmed by the gunboats of the Union forces in 1862. Fort Donelson anchored the Confederate strong point on the Cumberland River and was more strategically located on high ground in the town of Dover Tennessee. The Union Navy was unable to take this fort by water and the Union forces were forced to capture the area using land forces. Fort Henry is now underwater as a result of the damming of the Tennessee River in the 1940s, but Fort Donelson is a very popular tourist attraction for civil war enthusiasts and historians and has a large trench system which encompasses part of Dover Tennessee. In early

1934, President Roosevelt established the Tennessee Valley Authority, whose job it was to build dams to provide flood control and bring electricity to this rural area. About 800 families were relocated to the adjacent land and surrounding areas, this was accomplished using eminent domain laws at that time. My family is from the area which was known as Lost Creek and my father used to fish the Tennessee River and take part in what it was known as "Musseling" at that time. A hard worker could only make about a dollar a day by collecting mussel shells in the Tennessee River and so my father decided to join the Army in 1939. He was deployed to North Africa and then England to train troops for the invasion known as D-Day in 1944. My father had not been stateside since 1942 and he was wounded in the Ardennes Forest in 1944 just before what would be known as the Battle of the Bulge. In October,1944 my father was wounded in the hand with a German rifle grenade, and his hand became infected. Army surgeons were able to save his hand, and then he was assigned to escort a couple of soldiers who had lost their sight in combat, back to their home states. He arrived in San Francisco California and dropped off one of these blind soldiers and then escorted the remaining soldier to Louisiana by bus. At the end of these duties, he was given 60 days leave to return home and allow his hand to heal completely. As my father had not been home for four years, he was not familiar with the landscape of the area and asked the bus driver to put him off at the end of the bridge over the now completed Kentucky Lake. The bus driver informed my father that no one got off here, but fortunately a young girl seated near him said I know where he lives, and I will tell you where to drop him off. The young girl and my father spoke for a while and when the bus had gone a couple more miles, she indicated to the bus driver that this is where he needs to get off, "His family lives here Now". The kind young girl had instructed my father to get off at what is now known as the Fort Henry entrance to the Land Between the Lakes, as his family had been relocated to this area. My father walked for a couple of miles before stopping at a small store where they gave him directions to where his mother now lived. Indeed, this area had changed so much that it could not be recognized by a soldier who had lived there his entire life.

A second transformation was to occur for the Between the Rivers area in 1963, President Kennedy designated the "Land Between the Lakes" area as a national recreational area. A national recreation area differs from a national park in that guns would be allowed there for hunting and of course it would also be a fishing paradise, as well as a large camping area. For a second time residents of this area were told to relocate, using the eminent domain law. My family had just relocated to this area when my father retired from the Army in 1960. I became part of the second relocation, as I was a student in the first grade of a one room school known as Fort Henry School which had six grades being taught by a wonderful woman known as "Miss Sally Martin". Many of the residents of this area objected to this second relocation, but as this was an eminent domain relocation there was very little that they could do. There are some stories of residents who refused to leave this area and remained for some time. Some of these residents indicated that they would not leave and would only be taken at gunpoint, and to my knowledge none of these residents were ever threatened and simply left alone until they decided to leave the deserted area.

As part of the agreement for the residents who gave up their land, the Tennessee Valley Authority agreed that this area would never be developed, and no future communities would be allowed inside the LBL. In addition, it was agreed upon that no commercial industries would be allowed to move into this area. In 1998 transfer of control of the LBL was given to the USDA, Forestry Division, by Congress.

The LBL extends between Kuttawa Ky on the northern end to Dover Tennessee on the southern end. The area just below Kuttawa Ky comprises the upper peninsula of the LBL. The events that supposedly took place as related by this book, only concern the upper peninsula near Kuttawa Kentucky. The upper peninsula contains a canal which connects Lake Barkley to the Kentucky Lake. The author of this book does not conclude whether the events which took place on the upper peninsula are true or simply myth, these events are given as second and third hand accounts and some of these events are from retired law enforcement personnel. While some of these events are well documented in various blogs and on YouTube, you will not be able to obtain any public records which will corroborate their authenticity. This information is commonly known by many of the residents of this area, and it is usually said that if a story changes several times over a period of time it's a good indication that that story is myth. This story from the upper peninsula remains virtually unchanged for over forty years as related by the people who claim to have direct knowledge of the events. Indeed, if this story is true, the events would be so horrific as to sear a memory so completely that one would never be able to forget. It is said that these events were never given to the press and never publicized in any paper so that tourism and visitations to the Land Between the Lakes would not be affected. There are many beautiful places to visit in the Land Between the Lakes, including the bison pens where you can observe the buffalo much as they would've been in their natural habitats. Also, there is a planetarium along with a place called the Home Place that are worth visiting.

The Home Place is a re-creation of what it might have been like to have lived in the 1800s. There are many re-creations and demonstrations of the tools and artifacts of that time at the Home Place. The LBL has many campsites including Piney Campground and many primitive campsites in the lower and middle peninsula areas including facilities for large campers, with electrical hookups and water. At the very end of the upper peninsula there is evidence were campsites and hookups once existed but were removed, and much of this area has returned to wilderness.

Chapter 2

Undocumented Species

There are many interesting animal species that inhabit the LBL, some of these species have been introduced in recent years. As mentioned earlier, the bison was introduced to the LBL area many years ago in order to create a sustainable population. Coyotes are a dominant species in the LBL as they have wandered further eastward from their usual domains. The American Bald Eagle has established itself and there is a breeding population of these birds in all areas of the Land Between the Lakes. There is also at least one species of wolves and there are purported sightings of black panthers as well. When I was younger, I lived with my parents near what is now known as the Piney Campground, and my father and I were driving to Dover one day when a black panther ran across the path of our vehicle. My father slowed so as not to hit the animal and we both got a very good look at this panther. This panther could not be mistaken for any other species of cat because it was very big and had a long black tail, and this animal came up almost even with the hood of our 1956 Ford.

There are also several species of snakes in the LBL including copperheads, timber rattlesnakes, and cottonmouths. Scientists will tell you that these are the primary and only snakes that inhabit the LBL with the exception of possibly some pygmy rattlers. There may have been another species of snake in the Land Between the Lakes that scientists do not recognize as having ever existed.

My mother and father grew up in the area known as Lost Creek which is only about 3 miles from the Fort Henry entrance to the park. My parents related separate incidents to me about a snake that was commonly referred to as the "Hoop Snake" and I will start with my mother's experience with this snake. In 1938 my grandfather, who I was never fortunate enough to meet, was in the yard of their Lost Creek residence when he yelled for my mother to come assist him. When my mother approached him, he told her to not get too close and she could see that he had killed some kind of snake. He then told her to go get my grandmother so that she could look at the snake. He had noticed the snake at some distance before he said the snake grabbed a horn in its tail with its mouth and begin rolling toward him. He indicated that the snake would have hit him as it rolled directly toward him, except that at the last minute he dodged behind a tree. The snake at that very minute released the horn it had in its mouth and the horn struck that small tree. The snake had rolled much like a car tire that had been released to roll away on its own. My grandfather had been able to kill the snake with the garden hoe that he was using at the time in his garden.

The tree, which was about six inches in diameter, died several days later. As word of the snake that my grandfather had killed spread to neighbors, many came by over the next couple of days and looked at this peculiar species. Later my grandfather threw the remains of the snake into the nearby woods. The family had a dog at this time and unfortunately the dog had eaten some of the remains of the snake, and this dog got very sick and died.

My father related a story about the same kind of snake, but this incident occurred in Florida after he had joined the Army. He was on maneuvers near Jacksonville Florida in 1940 and he and another soldier had sighted the hoop snake about fifty feet in front of them. The snake had its tail in the air and protruding from the tail was a slightly curved spike. These soldiers remained motionless for several minutes and then started to move around the snake and as they did the snake's tail followed them. To explain this more thoroughly, the spike that was in the snake's tail followed the direction of their movements. Although this was the first time my father had seen this particular snake, his fellow soldier indicated he had seen these snakes before. This soldier stated that if we had gotten much closer the snake would have rolled toward us and the snake was using its horn to literally aim this rolling approach. I know the integrity of my parents, and if they indicated that they had observed these snakes then you could take this information as being fact. It is possible that these snakes are now extinct, and this is the reason there is no record of their existence. It is also possible that they are an undocumented species, that has simply not been recorded yet.

In recent years there have been a few new species of various insects and fish documented in the LBL area and it only makes sense that an area as large as this will have a great abundance of wildlife and possibly as yet documented animals. This is not to include the recently introduced animals such as the bison and the elk that currently inhabit this area. It is also possible that there are animals not known to science that may be aggressive predators and with such an abundance of deer, bison, and elk, this is certainly an area that would be attractive to such predators. There have been recent sightings of Black Panthers in this area and as mentioned earlier the sighting that my father and I had of this panther in 1963 leads me to believe that these animals have been here for a while. Black bears were at one time common to certain areas of the LBL, but none have been sighted in the area for years. If black bears were to enter the area, it would be necessary for them to cross several rivers, and some distance, which includes highly populated areas.

Permits are issued to those that want to hunt deer in the LBL, and many hunters take advantage of this opportunity. There are muzzleloader, bow, and regular gun seasons that are permitted within the LBL. Every year hunters enjoy a large harvest of both doe and buck deer, and as a consequence of the large-scale hunting in the LBL, hunters come in contact with many species of animals. There are a few purported contacts of animals that are as yet unidentified. Many of these contacts probably go unreported due to the possible harassment that one might incur if they spoke of these sightings.

There have been reports of hunters and hikers that go missing in the LBL area, and naturally in an area as large as the LBL there will be such reports and while many of these are solved there are a few cases that go unsolved.

Chapter 3

A Warning from the Shawnee Indians

In the early to mid-1700s many Shawnee Indians migrated west to the area now known as the Land Between the Lakes, and at this time there were many French trappers and hunters that were beginning to migrate into the area as well. For the most part there was a peaceful coexistence and cooperation between the Indians and trappers that inhabited this beautiful area. As these French trappers and other settlers began to migrate into this area a fur trade was established with the Shawnee Indians. As these trappers began to expand their territories further north into Kentucky the Shawnee Indians are said to have warned the trappers of certain areas that they should not enter. Many of these French trappers did not heed the warning and thought perhaps it was an effort to protect an even more abundant trapping area. It is reported that some of these trappers did not return from the area and were never heard from again.

At a time when explorers and trappers were first moving into the western expanses of what would become the United States it was not uncommon for people to go missing. Many accidents and natural phenomena including the weather could take the life of these industrious trappers. While there may have been small-scale search parties for an individual that went missing, there would not have been a modern-day search using helicopters, boats, and rescue squads. Many of these hunters and trappers that went missing would have been dismissed as the price that was paid for being an explorer in uncharted lands, as the resources did not exist at the time to do more thorough searches.

Indeed, this was a time where men fended for themselves, there was no welfare and nobody blamed anyone else for their condition, or circumstances. These men were tough as nails, and they carved paths through the wilderness and secured their own food sources. These early trappers and settlers, known as the "Long Hunters", endured hardships that we as modern people can only imagine.

The Shawnee Indians were attempting to warn the settlers and trappers of an animal the French trappers referred to as "Loup-Garou" the French translation being "Wolf-Man". Is it possible that the Shawnee Indians had encountered an unknown creature that was considered very dangerous? There is also a possibility that the Shawnee Indians had some crude agreement with these creatures so as not to enter these territories.

Very little documentation exists of these early periods in our history, but I believe the Indians of this time, possessed instincts and an understanding of nature that we cannot conceive. The Shawnee people had lived off the land for many years before moving west after having come in conflict with the Cherokee tribes. The territories of west Tennessee and Kentucky were indeed the new frontier in the early to mid-1700s, and these areas would become what is known as the Tennessee Valley.

There have been more recent reports of an animal that seems to stalk this area in the northern part of the LBL. In the late 1970s a young boy had received a new motorbike that he would take into the areas adjacent to his home. His parents lived near the Land Between the Lakes and it was not uncommon for him to take his motorbike into the upper Peninsula for rides along the many old roads and trails that still exist today. This area near Grand Rivers Kentucky is adjacent to the LBL, where the RV camping facilities used to be located and appear to have been removed. The young boy had a sister and older cousin that were visiting with them at the time. The young boy's sister and cousin heard the motorcycle at some distance coming toward the house. It was noted that the motorcycle was not changing speed and appeared to be wide open. In a short while the motorcycle became visible to the two children sitting on the front porch and they could tell that this was unusual because of the speed of the motorcycle. As a matter of fact, they were afraid he would miss the small road just outside the woods because he was going so fast and indeed the motorcycle landed several feet past the road after flying through the air. The young boy had let the motorcycle slide out from underneath him and seemed to be in a panic. While his older cousin and sister were trying to understand why the young boy was in a panic, they heard a scream from something in the woods. He began to tell them that something had grabbed him while riding his motorcycle in the woods. The young boy had tears ripped into the leg of his jeans, that had some blood oozing from the scratches which were visible through the torn jeans. He at that point had gathered his breath and said that it chased me and tried to grab me". A short while later something became visible just on the outskirts of the woods that looked to be tall and black in color. This event had happened a short time before dusk and a security light had just started to come on. This light was the commonly used mercury vapor security light that took a little while to reach full brightness. At that moment the children could see a large black figure standing on two legs that appeared to have the head of a dog or wolf. They quickly ran into the house and locked the doors and grabbed some kitchen knives and went to their mother's bedroom and hid under the bed. A short time later they could hear something walking on the porch and around the house and then they heard the sound of glass breaking, at almost the same moment they heard a car approaching and the horn began to blow, and they realized it was their mother coming home from grocery shopping. They did not move and could hear their mother coming into the house and calling for them as if annoyed. The mother was used to getting assistance with unloading the groceries from the car, and that is why she had blown the horn several times. The noise of the car approaching, and the horn blowing must have startled this creature which the mother had not seen. She found them in the bedroom under the bed in sheer panic and quickly learned why they had scuttled upstairs in terror. It was sometime later that their father arrived, and the story was related to him. He then related to them that he had seen a pile of bones up near the old sawmill, and then he instructed none of them to go into the woods again. This instruction was easily obeyed as the children had no desire to go near the woods again.

Another purported sighting which occurred in the 1970s was from a troop of Boy Scouts that was camped near the same area. This group of Boy Scouts along with their master had spotted a tall creature that stood on two legs and had what looked like a dog's snout on the other side of a stream and there was no explanation for what they had seen. These boy scouts concurred with what they had seen, along with the scout master of the troop.

Many people who venture into this area have reported the feeling that something was watching them from a distance, and almost all of these people indicate that they felt very uneasy and felt as if they were in great danger. There have been many cryptic researchers that have ventured into this area and also reported the same uneasy feelings. One of the many things that have been reported in this area and seems to coincide with these uneasy feelings is that the normal sounds of the forest are not detected during these incidents. No crickets are heard, no birds are heard, indeed it is almost complete silence. It is well documented when an apex predator enters certain areas that the normal sounds that you would hear in the forest are sometimes muted.

In 1993 a bow hunter was killed, and his tent was found to have been ripped open by an animal, and his bow was found broken in half. Witnesses who found his body indicated that he had been mauled, shredded, and partially consumed.

Several witnesses have reported an upright walking beast that many describe as a "werewolf" chasing them. A DNR officer is said to have reported some sort of animal that he could not explain that attacked and killed a man and women near a tent. He had tried to warn them of this creature's approach as he observed it stalking and then killing them. This officer was a little distance away from the shore in a fishing boat. The officer indicated that this had upset him so much that he just drifted for some time trying to wrap his head around what had just happened.

All of these sightings and reports seemed to come from very credible witnesses. The author recommends the book, "Beasts Between the Rivers" by Martin Groves, for a more detailed story of the bow hunter's death, and Mr. Grove's own experience, possibly on that same day. This book can be obtained on Amazon or through distributors.

For many years there have been reports of missing livestock and some of these livestock have been found with their throats torn out and many of the animals were eviscerated. It is also reported that portions of the animal had been eaten including the entrails and unidentifiable marks were also found on some of this these animals that could not be explained.

Since the introduction of buffalo to the area many buffalo calves have been found with similar marks and appeared to have been fed upon. There are also reports of buffalo being found in a defensive position guarding their young in the classic circular formation, and witnesses also state that these buffalo seemed very disturbed and uneasy. A massive animal the size of a buffalo would seem to have few predators unless it had been isolated and attacked by larger predators such as wolves.

There is an incident that occurred in the early 1973, that involved a group of Murray State University students. A group of six students decided to take a weekend vacation in the LBL on the upper end of the park. The students parked there VW micro bus and started a fire and gathered wood for the evening. The students were having a good time while downing a few beers when one of the students had to relieve himself. He then ventured a short distance into the woods and started to notice red eyes in the distance. He could then hear the scuffling of leaves all around in the nearby woods, and he also heard what sounded like a dog sniffing the air. Needless to say, the student hurried back to the campsite and told the others what he was hearing and a short time later the rest of the students begin to hear the shuffling in the woods. In addition to seeing multiple eye shines which appeared to be red, they could hear occasional low growling sounds. This was enough fun for them, and they quickly loaded back into the VW micro bus. As they took off, these students could see something chasing the vehicle and eventually catching them and making a loud noise at the back of the bus. The students witnessed a creature running on two legs with the head of a dog only much larger, about 3 to 4 times the size of a large dog's head. This creature was trying to hold on to the vehicle, and at that moment the student driving the bus floored the accelerator and was able to leave the area. These students did not stop until they were back on the campus of Murray State, where they parked their vehicle, to the great relief of the entire group. On the back of this vehicle, they could see four tears in the steel hood that houses the motor compartment. It is said that this group of students had no desire to go camping at the LBL campgrounds again.

A group of "rubbers" reported being chased out of this area, by a large dog that walked on two feet that was very aggressive. Tombstone rubbing has become a popular hobby for many, as they use wax paper, or rice paper and large crayons, or charcoal to preserve the writing of these old tombstones. These amateur historians help us preserve history that would otherwise be lost over time, and they do a great service in documenting the lives of the people that originally occupied this area. It is almost certain that many more incidents like this may go unreported, simply because people are afraid of the criticism that they might receive for reporting these incidents. Some of these encounters may involve people that simply go missing and may be far more gruesome in nature.

LBL as viewed from the Lower Peninsula

Chapter 4

A Breeding Population

Zoologists know that in order for a species to propagate and survive there are two requirements, one of these requirements is a sustainable food source. I can think of no better environment to provide the food source necessary for these creatures than the LBL. With an abundance of deer, elk and bison as well as several species of fish, there are very few areas in the world that would be a better habitat for a large predator such as this creature, this of course is assuming that these animals do not also survive by predication of humans, and there are a few of those around as well. The second requirement for this species to exist would be a breeding population, and there is some evidence from witnesses that this requirement has been fulfilled as well. The main highway through the Land Between the Lakes is known as the "Trace". A few years ago, a witness came forward who had traveled down this highway during the nighttime. The witness claimed to have seen a dog like creature walking on two legs crossing the road in the area of the upper Peninsula, and directly behind the creature were three smaller creatures identical to the one leading them. This witness described the creature as leading its pups across the road and was close enough to be able to hear the small creatures making "puppy sounds" only at a much lower pitch.

The history of this creature's existence in the LBL would seem to have been at least many centuries if not longer. With the reports from Shawnee Indians, and early settlers of this creature all the way through present day, then one could assume that there may be a sustainable population of this, as yet documented animal in the LBL.

A similar creature to the one described by witnesses in the LBL, may exist further north in Pennsylvania, there have been several witnesses, including one wildlife contractor, of a creature known as the "werewolf". This creature has been featured on the History channel show known as "Monster Quest"*. The descriptions of this creature are remarkably similar to what is commonly referred to as the "LBL Beast." The "Bray Road Beast" is another example of a creature with many sightings by seemingly credible individuals, that matches descriptions of the creatures seen in the LBL.

There are also reported sightings of a doglike beast in the swamp areas of Louisiana. There is one small island located in Louisiana that local residents know not to venture near, and they warn visitors not to go near this island especially at night. With the various sightings throughout the country including the Land Between the Lakes, it would seem that there may be a breeding population of an undocumented, dog like hominoid in many areas of the country. There are so many purported sightings of this creature that they are commonly referred to as the "Dogman".

* MonsterQuest America's Wolfman Caught on Film Season 4, Episode 9, A&E Television Networks Producers Doug Hajicek, Will Yates, Executive Producer
Dale Bosch October 31,2007

Chapter 5

The Massacre

The time of the massacre was early 1982 before the usual number of campers were present in the area of the upper peninsula campgrounds. This incident is believed to have occurred in early April and there would have still been a chill in the air as winter's last breath slowly faded. You will not be able to find stories in the newspapers during that period or tapes from television stations regarding this incident as it was never reported to the press, and these articles and news stories simply do not exist. What you will find is second-hand accounts of this incident reported in various blogs and on YouTube. If you do a search on Google or other search engines, you will also be able to find information on this incident.

Although there have been variations to a small degree in the events that occurred in 1982, these are mainly in details and the basic story remains the same for over 40 years. All of the events that purportedly occurred in the upper Peninsula come from either previous law enforcement officers, DNR officers or other state officials, that would have had personal knowledge of these events. These officials, for obvious reasons, wish to remain anonymous although in recent years as many of these officers grow old, they have been more open about their experiences. As the author mentioned previously in this book, I am simply presenting this information for your review, and I do not attest to the authenticity of this reported event. It is up to the individual reader to determine its validity. There have been some cryptid researchers that have been in the area of the upper peninsula recently and they have observed some unusual events and also have some video footage and photos. Some of these photos are included in this book for your observation.

The story of the massacre begins with a young couple calling the authorities in the small town of Grand Rivers, Kentucky using a pay phone. Please keep in mind this was 1982, there were no cell phones at that time, and even today, most areas of the LBL are not accessible by cell phone. The report is given to a couple of deputies in the Grand River's area, but the couple is visibly shaken and refuses to escort the deputies to the crime scene. This couple had discussed whether one would have stayed at the scene while the other would drive to the nearest pay phone, but that plan was quickly dismissed, as they were terrified by what they had seen. Instructions were given to the deputies as to how to get to this location at the campgrounds. This couple rented a hotel room and refused to go back into the LBL area. These deputies quickly dispatched information on the radio as would be standard procedure and on arrival the deputies and several other emergency units observed a camper with a campfire very near that was beginning to dwindle. Upon further inspection the horrible scene was about to unfold. As other emergency units begin to arrive, including an ambulance, it became very apparent that the services of the ambulance would not be needed as the family of this camper was deceased, as a matter fact this family was VERY DECEASED. The campfire was stoked, and the wood was replenished to assist with lighting the scene, and at this time, many emergency units begin arriving at the scene, including state police. It is unclear when the first coroner arrived at the scene, but it is said that there would be a total a total of six coroners at this grisly crime scene with some of these physicians coming from out of state. One specific coroner was said to have been from Memphis Tennessee. Upon closer inspection the father of this family was found in front of the camper, he had been dismembered with both arms missing and seemingly tossed to each side. The father's head was barely attached to his body and twisted so as to face almost backwards. There were unusual marks on his body and there was a lot of speculation as to what animal may have done this. One of the deputies asked a coroner, "Was this the work of a bear or pack of wolves?" The coroner simply replied by shaking his head. A short distance from the father a young boy about eleven years old was found near the entrance to the camper door and it seemed evident that this young boy had seen what was happening to his father and was trying to make his way back into the camper.

The camper door had several rips in the metal covering and one hinge had been ripped from the camper door and it was hanging on the remaining hinge. There were similar marks on this young boy as those found on the father. The scene inside the camper was one that not even a horror story would rival. The mother of this family had apparently put up as good a fight as possible, but this fight was obviously a futile one. It is said that many of the emergency personnel that arrived on the scene, including the deputies, had retched almost uncontrollably. The author of this book was an EMT with a rescue squad for many years and for these well-trained emergency personnel to have problems with an accident scene or crime scene is unusual. The men of law enforcement are used to dealing with automobile accident scenes, some of which can be pretty horrific.

It is said that the inside of the camper had several rip marks in the walls and one of the deputies thought this might have been done with a knife but there seemed to be a pattern to these rips that looked like those of a very large hand that had raked the walls of the camper. There was a putrid smell emanating from the entire crime scene but particularly inside the camper and this smell possibly contributed to some of the emergency personnel becoming sick.

The mother of this family was severely mutilated, eviscerated and blood was splattered throughout the inside of the camper and as the father and son's bodies had exhibited, there were deep bite marks on her upper body.

During the initial stages of the investigation, it was thought that these were the only victims of this horrific crime, but upon entering the very back room of this camper some small clothing for a young girl was discovered. There was a renewed hope that there may have been a survivor to this vicious attack and search parties were dispatched to comb the surrounding woods. At this time the rescue squad and several others had arrived and were quickly dispatched to search the immediate area. The deputies that had taken the initial report began searching the area as well and after they had traveled a relatively short distance moving cautiously the entire way, one of the deputies began hearing something drip on his hat. At this point he then looked up and saw a young girl about 30 feet in the air hung on a limb. He let out a scream which quickly attracted other emergency personnel and it is said that he began to whimper at the site he was beholding. A young girl had been lodged in a tree with her hand almost severed and she was dripping blood. This is what had hit the deputies hat. This young girl appeared to have been "eaten on", by some unknown predator. She had been placed in the tree much like a cheetah will place its kill up high in a tree, so that the prey may be peacefully feed upon. It was estimated that this girl was about nine years old at the time of her death, by those on the scene. There are no public records that would give the ages of this girl, or the rest of her family.

One can only imagine what went through the mind of this poor young girl as she was being violently pulled out of this camper, after having seen her mother killed in a vicious way by a creature that should not exist. This young girl had probably been told after having a nightmare, as most children do, that creatures like this are only in our dreams. Indeed, this whole nightmarish attack would shake the beliefs of anyone who had to experience it. The one redeeming factor of this whole incident is that it would have been over very quickly as this creature was probably able to dispatch the entire family within minutes.

The coroner that had been examining the father's body had noticed marks on the father's back. These claw marks almost looked like bear claw marks except there were significant differences. These claw marks were larger than that of a bear and also there was an opposing digit. These marks looked to of been made by an almost human looking hand with claws, only much larger. Four of the claw marks had deeply

penetrated the father's back with the thumb digit leaving a lesser penetration into his back. A short time later as these doctors were collecting the evidence, one of the father's arms was collected and bagged, and at this time a dark colored fur
was discovered in the father's death grip. In addition to this evidence, this same fur was collected from the tree where the young girl had been found. This fur was later analyzed using DNA techniques that became available and found to be that of an unknown hominid with the closest match being that of Canis Lupus, a wolf.

The author is told by a reliable source, and retired law enforcement officer, that a record exists in Lyon County Ky, of this family's demise but if you attempt to obtain this record, you will be met with great hostility.

Chapter 6

Federal Authorities Take Control

The young couple that discovered the bodies of the campers and had called authorities had indicated that it was just past dusk when they discovered this horrific site, and it was estimated that these deaths occurred right around sunset of the that evening. It appeared as though the father and son had been working outside of the camper and the mother and daughter were inside the camper at the time this creature approached the campsite. Some of the personnel on site had noticed that the father and mother had a musky cologne, and perfume, respectively, and speculated that this could have possibly attracted this animal. At some time, early the next morning federal authorities are said to have moved in and told all local authorities to establish a perimeter on the outside of the park and the park was closed. All personnel that had been on site were told not to tell anyone of the events of the previous night and were allowed to leave. It is said that in addition to these federal authorities a group of soldiers arrived that morning probably from nearby Fort Campbell KY. This group of soldiers may have been from the famous 101st Airborne division, or possibly some other special forces unit. What is clear is that witnesses observed men in military uniform on this crime scene, with military equipment and armament. The local officials and state police established perimeters around the entrance to the park as they had been instructed. Although the exact time is unclear, it is reported that the officers that were on the perimeter of the park heard the simultaneous reports of several automatic weapons emanating from inside the park, and at some distance. It is reported that some of the DNR officials that had been on site that evening had then been allowed to return to the park and assist the authorities. These witnesses observed about eight soldiers struggling to load a foul-smelling creature with the head of a dog, onto a flatbed truck, or military truck. This was probably what in the military is commonly referred to as a "deuce and a half truck". It is said that this animal took up almost the entire bed of this military truck with the exception of a few inches. The witnesses stated that this creature was covered in dark fur and had the head of a dog that was about two or three times in size of what a large dog's head would be. The soldiers had tracked this animal to a dugout cave some distance away from the initial crime scene and engaged the creature at the mouth of this small cave. This creature had claws about two inches long and a body similar to that of a man, with the torso being very muscular. This description would seem to fit most of the purported sightings of what is commonly referred to as the Dogman. It is stated that a large portion of this animals' chest had been blown out due to the weaponry that had been used to kill it. The odor which emanated from this creature was said to be that of something dead and very similar to the odor which had been encountered inside the camper.

To the author's knowledge, this is the only purportedly documented case of a family being killed by such a creature, although it may be suspected that more families may have perished at the hands of these beasts. If these creatures do indeed occasionally feed on humans, there may be very little evidence left. There have been witness sightings of large piles of bones in this general area and while most of these bones are those of deer and other animals, it is possible that a few of these bones could be human. Predatory animals such as hyenas are known to collect and stack the bones of their victims for consumption at a later time.

The author ran a bait shop at the Hwy. 79 entrance of the LBL when this event would have taken place, and I can confirm the park closed for one day which is highly unusual. More than one person stopped by my bait shop coming back from the LBL and asked me if I knew why the park was closed, this was early April of 1982, but this event occurred over 40 years ago, and I cannot recall the exact date. The first time I heard the story of the events that purportedly occurred in the LBL was in 1998 through word of mouth, however at the time I was somewhat skeptical.

1980's "Deuce and a Half" Standard Military truck used for many years.

Clawed footprint from the LBL
Photo courtesy of Dewey Edwards

Chapter 7

Anatomy of a Killer

If one had the abilities of God and could design a perfect killing machine, you would probably start with the descriptions of this creature. Those who have witnessed this creature around the country and the LBL describe it as being somewhere between seven feet and nine feet tall and weighing about four to six hundred pounds. Although heights and weights are sometimes hard to judge especially if you are being pursued by such a creature, it is apparent that this is not a small animal. Black bears, which once inhabited this area could reach a maximum of 450 pounds with a height of about 6 1/2 feet when standing on their hind legs and although black bears would have a similar snout as that described on this creature, it is well known that these bears are not very agile on two legs. It is also highly unlikely that if black bears have migrated into this area that credible witnesses would confuse them with another animal.

One witness who described himself as a federal agent on a stakeout claims to have witnessed this creature running across a field and grabbing a white tail deer. The equipment that the federal agent was using indicated that this creature had achieved a speed of forty-seven miles per hour. It would seem that in some instances where witnesses are chased by this creature that it is simply trying to remove them from its territory. If this creature is able to reach speeds in excess of forty miles per hour and weighs five hundred pounds it is not likely that a human could escape its pursuit, should it decide to prey upon them. It is also unlikely that there would be much evidence left by this creature of any human predication that might occur.

The majority of witnesses describe this creature's upper body as being very muscular, much like that of professional weightlifter, with muscular arms and torso, only much larger. Descriptions of the lower parts of the animal include muscular thighs with human like legs and feet with claws that extend from the toes. This creature's arms are described as being longer than those of humans with large hands and digits that terminate into claws. The claws of this creature have been described as being between about one to three inches with two inches seeming to be the average. The average size of a black bear claw is one to two inches and that of a grizzly is two to four inches. Needless to say, black bears and grizzlies do enormous damage to the human body when they either attack or prey on people.

To complete the perfect killing machine, one will equip this creature with the senses of a wolf. The ability to smell prey at great distances is well documented in dogs and particularly in wolves and blood hounds. Zoologists know that grey wolves have one-hundred times the sense of smell as that of humans. This great sense of smell allows them to be aware of any animals that might enter their territory long before most other animals can detect them. Humans would stand very little chance of seeing this creature or even knowing it is present should it decide to stalk them.

Many years ago, during World War 1, there is an account of a soldier that was killed and returned to a location not far from the LBL. The soldier had been wounded in combat and later died and was returned by ship from the European battlefields. The family had been notified of the soldiers return but as the case sometimes happened during this period of time, soldiers were sometimes misidentified and sent to the wrong localities. The family had wondered if this would be the case with their son and if the body in the sealed box would be that of their son. Soon after the arrival of their son's remains, the family made their way to the church where the funeral would be held, and they were accompanied by the soldier's dog. It is said when they arrived at the church the dog went to the casket and smelled it and immediately collapsed on the floor. This dog was mourning his master who had perished in "The Great War". The actions of this dog were all the proof that these parents would need to know that their son had been returned to them. This dog lived for several years and never left the grave of their son, as the family would provide food for his dog to a location near that grave. When this dog died, he was buried next to his master to whom he had remained loyal for his entire life.

A dog's sense of smell is almost unrivaled in the animal world. Domestic dogs are used for many purposes such as cadaver dogs, drug sniffing dogs, and tracking dogs. Even with modern technology, we as humans have not been able to achieve the abilities of these animals by artificial means.

As you recall, the Murray State students that camped at LBL all reported hearing "sniffing sounds" from the surrounding woods, so it would seem that these animals rely on sense of smell to a great extent.

In summary, some of these animals could weigh as much as two offensive linemen, travel at speeds in excess of forty miles an hour and have tremendous strength with the claws of a black bear. There is one more aspect of this animal that some witnesses have observed. This animal, much like dogs will do, has been observed grabbing its prey by the neck and shaking it with its mouth thus breaking its neck with rapid motion. Those who own dogs have observed them in playful moods grabbing their stuffed toys and shaking them vigorously. This technique is instinctive in dogs, wolves, and all canines, and is indeed a very effective and deadly method of disabling another animal.

What appears to be a partial clawed print
recorded by Hellbent Holler in 2022 near
the massacre site.

Thermal image captured by Hellbent Holler researchers, if you look closely near the uprooted tree in the center of picture, you will see what appears to be an upright figure with long arms and dog like ears.

Chapter 8

The Alpha Wolf

Biologists have observed Wolf behaviors for many years and have categorized their behaviors according to pack behavior. The alpha wolf, and its mate are of course the leader of the wolf family pack. The beta wolf is the subordinate to the alpha wolf and considered the lieutenant of the pack, and his job is to take over if the alpha wolf is injured or killed and continue leading and protecting the pack. The omega wolf is the least wolf of the pack and is subordinate to the rest of the family. It would seem logical that these animals would follow a similar hierarchy to that of the wolf packs. Dispersal is the term used by biologists which refers to a wolf that leaves the pack because it no longer has the physical ability to compete with the alpha dog. Sometimes the alpha dog becomes unable to lead the pack and may disperse from the pack to become a lone wolf. It might be possible that the animal that attacked these campers was a lone wolf and not part of the pack. Lone Wolf's are known to coexist along the borders of wolf packs respecting their territory and yet fending for themselves. It should not be impossible for human DNA and wolf DNA to produce an offspring that would be part human and part wolf. The closest primates to humans are orangutans, and they share about 98.8% of human DNA, yet it is impossible for orangutans and humans to breed. This seemingly impossible creature might share the intelligence of a human with the primal instincts of the wolf pack family. New techniques in DNA technology are being discovered almost on a daily basis. Some scientists are now using a technique known as environmental DNA collection, and there have been samples collected from the northwestern areas of the United States, that have detected an unknown primate that has 99.8% human DNA. This technique is accomplished by taking samples of streams and ponds and other sources to detect what creatures have been there. It is not possible for human contamination to create DNA that is 99.8% human, if a DNA sample is contaminated and mishandled you simply have 100% human DNA. There is still much to be learned in the genetics field and new discoveries and techniques are yet to come.

Assuming that we have an animal that roams the upper peninsula of the LBL that is part primate and part wolf, it might be possible to collect these environmental samples to confirm its existence. If the witnesses that have come forward with the apparent DNA evidence that exists for this creature are legitimate, it may be possible that we have a primate similar to human with wolf attributes living in the LBL. This attack was supposedly kept from the press and covered up by the federal government, so there could be evidence filed away somewhere in the vaults of the US government that could verify this unknown creature's lineage. It might even be possible that this creature has more in common with the great apes rather than humans. And who is to say that this creature might not have some of the DNA that is possessed by the well-known " Bigfoot" creatures.

The TV show on the "History Channel" known as " Monster Quest", documented an unknown DNA from a creature that had been disturbing a remote fishing cabin on an island near Canada. * This evidence had been collected using a nail trap which is basically a board that has nails or screws protruding from it. This trap was placed on the porch of a cabin that had been breached by what was thought to be a bear. This unknown primate sample DNA shared about 99.8% of human DNA, with one "Ape" marker, and was believed to have been that of a Bigfoot creature.

In 1982, DNA science would not be available but other techniques were that would help identify unknown samples. DNA discoveries were made in 1989, that would change science and allow for more precise identification of tissue samples. The alleged sample that was taken would be even more valuable today if it were available. Hopefully more interest in this area of the LBL, will bring scientists to the area, for Environmental DNA testing.

* MonsterQuest Sasquatch Attack Proven by DNA Season 1 Episode 2, A&E Television Networks Producers Doug Hajicek, Will Yates, Executive Producer Dale Bosch October 31,2007.

This is the ravine that the creature is believed to have traveled to the camper before the attack.

Chapter 9

First Word of the Incident

It was early in the morning, about 3 AM in early April 1982 when two deputies arrived at a local convenience store in the Grand River's Kentucky area. The witness that worked at the store could tell that these deputies were visibly upset. One of the deputies had left the store and is said to have "thrown up" not too far from the gas pumps. It is said that these deputies would not say much when they first arrived and purchased some coffee. After some time had gone by the clerk joined the deputies on a bench outside of the store as it was early in the morning and business was slow. This witness said at first the deputies were just saying they could not believe what they had seen but eventually, they begin the give more details of what they had seen. It is said that as the deputies begin to talk to each other and with the store clerk, this horrible scene was unfolded to her. The story of the slain family and their daughter that had been found hanging from the tree at the nearby campsite shocked this witness. One can understand how these deputies who had just been on the site of such a horrific crime would need to get this off their chest. This young lady's story would be the first piece of information that was made public as the events of the that evening were detailed in her writings. One can only imagine how she had listened to every word that these deputies had to say with such intensity as each detail was revealed. This witness seems to be very credible and would have no reason to make up such a horrible story. Indeed, stories such as this, only seem to come from the mind of someone such as Stephen King. As the years passed by this story slowly becomes a cold case and since it was not published or seen on the local news, it simply fades to obscurity or is dismissed as folklore. It is only later when law enforcement officers and witnesses that would have been on site retire, does this story begin to reappear. Many of these officers and officials feel an obligation to this poor family that perished on that fateful evening and have come forward to confirm the events that occurred in that campground. For many years these officials have kept this information to themselves as they were instructed and some of them, I am sure, feared for their jobs, as they had family obligations. In many instances these purported witnesses confirm the events of the massacre or simply state that it did indeed happen. One fact is certain, and that is that if the events recounted by these witnesses are indeed true this would have been seared into their memories, so that they would never forget.

There are some researchers that claim that as many as twelve to eighteen lives have been lost in this area over the last forty years, although many of these incidents are hard to document.

The campsites that were in this area included electricity and running water as well as restroom facilities and showers. A metal gate has been placed blocking entrance to the area that once harbored these beautiful campsites. It is still possible for campers to go into these areas and to erect tents in these primitive campsites, however you do so at your own risk. It seems almost as if the authorities do not want to acknowledge that there are any dangers in this area but at the same time do not promote this area. Some witnesses have indicated that if you ask a Ranger or park authority whether it is okay to camp in this area, they will simply say you can but will not elaborate on directions or other information. This hands-off approach seems to be common for the remote campsites that are located behind the gate that blocks the access road. This road is not maintained beyond this gate to the author's knowledge but one can drive to this gated area and walk into the area, there is a graveyard that dates back to the 1700's that is located near this gated area.

Cemetery near the massacre site

Chapter 10

A Possible Witness to the Massacre

Recently, at the time of the writing of this book, a witness has come forward who claims to have been with the family that perished in the LBL campground in 1982. Although I cannot either confirm or deny his claims, this witness seems to be credible and has many more details of this purported incident. The witness claims that he was a friend of the family and even provides the names of the family and some details about their past. The witness who calls himself Roger says that the family that perished on the evening of April 7th was an Amish family that for one reason or another had left the Amish community which was located in Indiana. Roger provides the names of the family as follows: Levi was the father, Diane was the mother, with two children Stephen and Connie. Roger was 15 years old at the time of the attack on the camper. Roger describes the camper model as being a 1982 Holiday Imperial camper. Although some of the details he gives differ from the well-known story of the incident, his story would seem to qualify the actual event itself. Roger claims that shortly after their arrival at the campsite, the family was attacked by one or possibly two creatures which he described as looking like tall men with a head of a large canine. Roger and Eli were able to shoot the creature with 410- and 20-gauge shotguns, respectively. Eli did not survive the creature's attack, but Roger said that he rolled underneath the camper and hid in the compartment which houses the driveshaft of the vehicle. Roger describes the muffled attack he heard, that took place inside the camper, which he says killed Connie and Diane. Roger is not certain that there were two creatures but suspects that the almost simultaneous sound which came from the rear of the camper indicated the presence of a second creature. He had also heard Diane exclaim, "It's coming through the window". After approximately fifteen minutes, Roger then ran to the main road or the "Trace" and was able to hitch a ride with a farmer in a blue Ford pickup. Roger saw only a brief glance of the creature that attacked Eli and Stephen and said he was able to get a shot off at the creature that attacked them. He states that as his round hit this creature, it collapsed but quickly regained its footing.

Roger's account of this well-known story differs in a couple of key points which he emphasizes. Roger indicates that the daughter, Connie, was found behind the camper and that the creature itself was found hanging in the tree. Roger also claims that he returned to the scene with a federal agent after some period of time and provided more information to law enforcement officials that were still on the scene. The second difference from the original accounts of the tragedy was in the level of severity of the attacks. Roger indicated that the bodies were not as dismembered as described by other witnesses and this creature, or creatures were simply more efficient in biting and breaking the necks of the victims. He describes the scene as still being "very bad". Roger also states that these attacks were over very quickly and took only moments.

Roger seems very disturbed by the fact that there was no accounting for the family remains, and he has a very valid point. What became of this poor family, are they buried in a nearby cemetery? Roger indicates that there would have been no problem identifying this family as they had current license plates and there was more documentation inside the camper that would tell who they were. The second question is what happened to this family's possessions, their camper was certainly a newer model as well as the 1982 Chevette that Roger claims was being towed behind this camper. Rogers sixth sense tells him this family may be buried somewhere close to this area or possibly their ashes were scattered somewhere around a nearby cemetery. A forty-year-old cold case such as this would be hard to investigate, and if this poor family had close relatives, it is possible that they were simply told the family died in a horrible automobile accident, and their bodies returned in closed caskets. One can only speculate at this point in time as to what happened to their remains, property and what any relatives may have been told.

Roger has also stated that there were some military vehicles on site when he had returned to the scene, and he speculated that these may have been National Guard troops, but he could not be certain. Roger's account would seem to confirm that some branch of the military became involved with this incident. Although some of the account that he brings forth differs from other witnesses that claim to have been at the scene of this horrible tragedy, it is similar enough to add a touch of credibility to this story.

There may have been two separate incidents that occurred in slightly different locations, that involved two separate families, and two different campers. Another incident which may further describe the story, which has been related over the years, involved a towed camper. This family coincidentally involved four family members that may have been attacked by an unknown creature's and slaughtered in a similar fashion and this event may have occurred within two months of this well-known story. With such a long period of time having passed and witnesses who remain silent for so long it is virtually impossible to distinguish whether this was one event or possibly two events.

The sheer number of sightings during this period of time of the late 1970's and early 1980's might indicate that two separate events were entirely possible. The story in this book of the massacre that occurred in the early 1980's could possibly have been completely unrelated to Roger's account.

Chapter 11

In the Presence of Beasts

If you have ever been hunting or just enjoy the outdoors and the sounds sites and beauty of nature, then you may well have become accustomed to the presence of birds and other wild animals that inhabit the forest. Those who venture into the woods, even if these are small patches of trees near their house, learn to listen to the many beautiful sounds of nature that seem to form their own orchestra. Those individuals that are confined to large cities and the smells of modern civilization may not be able to appreciate these excursions into the woods that many of us enjoy on a regular basis. The author, having been fortunate enough to grow up in a rural area, has enjoyed the beauty, sights, and sounds of this wonderful orchestra. Those who have a yearning to go camping and travel great distances to enjoy the outdoors also have this great yearning in their souls. I have been fortunate enough to live in rural areas as well as large cities and I can tell you in less than a moment which setting I prefer. After you have ventured into the woods many times you become comfortable with the sounds and sights of nature and other than checking your footing for creatures that you do not wish to become acquainted with, i.e. snakes, there is generally a feeling of comfort and well-being. It is true that tics, mosquitoes, and flies are the parts of nature that can be most annoying while walking through the woods, but this is just considered the price you pay for freedom and relaxation. As a general rule you have very little to fear from animals while walking through the woods with the exception of coyotes in certain areas while areas further west have populations a bear and cougar many people still enjoy the pleasure of hiking trails and bike trails.

My personal preference is to be armed when I venture into the woods as this gives me some comfort and confidence should I encounter a rabid animal or other predator that I do not wish to face with a big stick. Birds may fly as you walk, and squirrels may scurry away and occasionally a rabbit may run out of the thicket and startle you, but this is generally expected and not alarming while walking in the wild.

Hunters know that a wounded animal can be very dangerous, and this is why experienced hunters know not to immediately chase the deer that they have just shot, but simply wait a period of time and track the trail that this deer leaves. It is said that more people are killed by deer than any other wild creature and while it is always nice to see deer in the wild, one should know that these are creatures that are capable of fending for themselves. Anyone who has been squirrel hunting knows that while these are tiny creatures, after you shoot one with your shotgun or .22 rifle you make sure to you use the butt of your gun to ensure these creatures are no longer conscious. There has been more than one instance of an inexperienced hunter reaching down to grab his prey and experiencing the sensation of 1/2 inch incisors tearing into their hand. All animals have natural instincts for survival, including humans. Though we sometimes become accustomed to our surroundings and plentiful food sources and technology one should never forget that we are indeed just another animal in the forest.

Those who had wandered into the woods sometimes have a different experience than the usual pleasant trip that most people enjoy, and this experience is not what they ever desired or wanted unless they happen to be cryptic researchers. Witnesses who have experienced these unnerving trips back to nature all have certain descriptions of their surroundings which seemed to coincide with the presence of an apex predator. Many people experience an eerie silence in the woods with the absence of crickets, bird song, and the general activity you would normally hear from the many creatures of the wild. Another reported abnormality is the occasional sense of being watched and observed. We have many senses that we do not understand, and these senses are probably derived from earlier generations of our ancestors who had to fend for themselves. Peripheral vision is one of the most useful senses that we have, as many witnesses have stated that they see black images flash across the woods while in the presence of these Dogmen.

Anyone who hunts deer knows that deer often walk with their heads forward and use their peripheral vision to detect any motion to their sides. Experienced hunters are aware of a deer's uncanny ability to see motion at relatively great distances and make their movements as gently as possible to prevent spooking these deer.

Another commonly reported trait of these Dogmen is that they seem to communicate using what sounds like a dog whistle sound. These animals seem to hunt in small packs and many witnesses have reported the sound of whistles coming from several directions and eventually surrounding them. This animal may also be an opportunistic hunter choosing individuals for predication and avoiding humans in large groups. Those who are lucky enough to avoid these animals and sense their presence are the lucky ones, as stated earlier in this book there are several reported cases of individuals who have chosen to camp alone who simply go missing. Sometimes the only evidence that is found is usually in the form of tents that have been ripped apart, and in some instances, human remains that have been partially eaten. In some cases where more than park officials are aware of an event that has taken place which involves a death, it seems as though the general release of information to the public is that someone was killed by an unknown animal, or coyotes. One fact seems certain, if these creatures do exist and there seems to be an abundance of evidence supporting this, they are far more likely to know you are around well before you detect them, and with speeds in excess of 40 miles an hour while running on all fours you are not likely to escape their vicious attack unless you are armed.

Chapter 12

Dogman, Bigfoot, and Other Stories

Throughout history there have been many sightings of Bigfoot creatures, as well as Dogmen. One event which was reported to have occurred involved the famous frontiersman, Daniel Boone. The story was passed on from Boone to his associates shortly after the event occurred. Boone and his son were hunting in Ohio near what would eventually become the city of Cincinnati when they encountered what he described as an 11-foot-tall ape-like creature. His son was the first to see this creature and had fired two musket shots into its chest, to no effect. The creature then picked Boone's son up and slammed him to the ground and it is at that moment Boone came to his son's aid. Before the creature reached down a second time to pick his son up this creature sighted Boone and turned his way. Boone, being the crack shot that he was leveled his musket at the creature and shot it through the eye which felled the creature immediately. Although his son was hurt but still able to walk, Boone took time to examine this creature. He noticed after using his knife to cut the chest of the creature partially open, that this creature had a solid breastplate that encompassed its chest. This solid breastplate was about an inch thick and curved around the body of this creature much as human ribs curve around the chest of a man.

Another account of an incident which occurred in a North Carolina area near the mountainous regions of the border with Tennessee involves both Bigfoot and Dogman creatures. Many years ago, an older gentleman who owned some land in this area had become accustomed to the sight of both Bigfoot creatures as well as Dogmen. He did not bother them, and they did not bother him even though he was aware that they were around his property. One evening he heard a commotion outside of his home and walked to the edge of the woods where he had a view of what was making the noise. This man stated that he saw a fight between a large Bigfoot and a large Dogman. Surrounding this fight were Dogmen on one side and other Bigfoot creatures opposite of them. It seems as though these creatures were trying to settle a dispute between them, possibly a territorial dispute which had arisen. The man also noticed a small Bigfoot near this area which appeared to be dead. He stated that the two creatures fought for a while and then almost as if taking a break went to their appropriate sides for a short rest as if almost in a refereed boxing match. The man stated that the Bigfoot was getting the worst of this fight and appeared almost exhausted. When the two creatures came back together to fight, he stated that the Bigfoot became enraged and came down with his fist with all his weight on top of the Dogman's head. He stated that he could hear the Dogman's legs break and snap and then the bigfoot creature picked up a rock and brought it down on the Dogman's head. He then stated that both groups slowly left the area in opposite directions as if a contest had been settled by the two creatures. The size of the Dogman and the Bigfoot indicated that these were probably the leaders of their clans, and the Dogman would have most certainly have been the Alpha dog.

There are many accounts of disputes between these two creatures, and it was widely believed that as a general rule the two creatures tolerate each other but do not get along. And one can suspect that there are probably many different territorial disputes that are settled in mortal combat between the leaders of these creatures. Credible witness reports from the LBL indicate that in some instances these creatures may work in tandem to gather prey. Martin Groves book "Beast Between the Rivers", has more details about these two creatures possibly cooperating and hunting together.

Several eyewitness accounts of encounters with these Dogmen indicate that these are very intelligent creatures. One witness account describes staring at one of these creatures and having the feeling that this creature was calculating what his next move would be. It is a well-known fact that if a predator senses that it has an advantage over its prey, then it will attack. Advice is often given to people who encounter bears to stand up as tall as possible and make noises in an attempt to make this bear leave you alone. There are accounts of dogmen being shot with smaller caliber guns to little effect and from other witness accounts, these creatures seem to understand that a gun is a weapon that can do them harm. In many cases witnesses report that these creatures stalk and surround them in a very coordinated and orchestrated manner. As noted earlier in this book, it appears as though these creatures communicate through whistles or other forms of communication.

The author's son had an encounter with a bigfoot creature near the small town of Westmoreland, Tennessee which is located north of Nashville at the Kentucky border. This area has had many sightings of Bigfoot creatures throughout the years. When my son was younger, I had taught him how the squirrel hunt and gave him a 20-gauge shotgun for his birthday. My son would go into the woods behind our house and squirrel hunt with the stipulation that he could not go beyond the next ridge so that he could be heard in the event of a problem. He did this quite often and had no fear of the woods and bagged many squirrels near our home. My parents lived across the road, and they had an almost hollow tree that my son was hitting with a broken stick, and he began to hear something making a lot of noise on the next ridge behind their house. To his astonishment, my son saw a large bipedal creature covered in dark fur running on this ridge about 75 yards from him. The creature appeared to veer toward him momentarily but continued on its path through the woods, but this convinced my son that he should seek shelter. He began pounding on his grandmother's back door and when she opened the door, he immediately shut it and locked it. After he gathered his breath, he told her what he had seen, and she said that he was "white as a sheep". He never had trouble going into the woods and squirrel hunting prior to this event, however for the next few years he would not venture into the woods.

Researchers currently believe that Bigfoot creatures communicate to each other by using limbs to pound on trees and it is also possible that this may be a form of distress call that enables them to communicate over long distances.

A more recent purported event occurred in the small town of Bumpus Mills Tennessee where the author lives and involves the apparent attack of a Dogman. A woman who recently lost her husband had acquired two rottweilers to help protect her home and give her some comfort and company. She loved these animals and took good care of them and had let them out one evening in her fenced yard so that they might take care of their business. She began to hear the dogs growl at a lower-than-normal tone, and this caught her attention. She then ventured onto her back porch where she could see these dogs growling and intensely watching the end of the fence which was not illuminated well. Soon after she heard the growls of the dogs, she heard a much lower growl with greater intensity that lasted longer. The dogs sensed her presence on the porch and soon thereafter began to run to the area where the low rumbling growl emanated from. She could see what appeared to be an arm come out from this area and grab one of her dogs and soon the dog was whining in pain and a short time later, the other dog was tossed over 30 yards to the other side of the fence. This dog was clearly hurt but begin to limp back to the aid of the other dog and was quickly dispatched. Both of these Rottweilers weighed over 130 pounds. The woman had thought this might have been a prank by her son-in-law until she reached him on the phone shortly before the attack and realized that this was no joke. Shortly thereafter the son-in-law who lives very close drove his truck close to the backyard with his high beams on high and at this moment the woman and her son-in-law saw this creature clearly. She had a bird feeder that was 10 feet high and this creature which had the head of the Wolf and was standing on two legs came to a height about 1 foot below the height of the bird feeder. Her son-in-law emptied his shotgun into the creature, but it still stood holding in its hands one of the rottweilers that it was in the process of consuming while standing with one leg on the other rottweiler. The son-in-law at that point emptied his 10 mm handgun into this creature which finally made it run out of the backyard. This poor woman called the sheriff during this period and shortly thereafter the sheriff approached the property and saw what he thought was a bear holding its young running across the road. After the sheriff spoke with the woman and surveyed the scene, he then realized that the dog that the creature had been standing on had been taken when this creature fled the scene thus dropping the already half eaten dog in its hands. The sheriff dispatched more deputies to the scene, and he began to patrol nearby roads in this rural area. Shortly after the sheriff began his patrol, he spotted the creature again and stopped his car and leveled his rifle at the creature and shot two rounds and was certain he hit the creature. The creature ran off for a second time and shortly thereafter the sheriff found the partially consumed Rottweiler which this creature had dropped.

Another terrifying Incident occurred near the North Stewart Forest not too far from the Cross Creeks area of Tennessee and involved a camper. Tim a very experienced hunter and ex-military veteran decided to go black powder hunting In this area which is fairly close to the LBL area. Tim set up a very nice camp and intended to go deer hunting the next day when in the middle of the night he was awakened by a horrible scream that he had never heard before. This noise that awakened him was very close to his tent and he described it as a horrible scream much louder than any normal animal that would be present in the woods. Being a trained military veteran, Tim is not the kind of person that would be startled easily but the rest of the night he huddled close to his gun and never went back to sleep. He indicated that he is familiar with the sound of a screech owl, and this was not one. The scream vibrated his tent and his body as well and would have come from a much larger creature. Tim decided to pack up his camp the next day and hunt another day. He has only been back to the area in the daytime and will not camp in this location at night.

Another incident happened in Indian Mound Tennessee and involved Dylan who was at his father in-law's house. This incident occurred around 10 pm one night, as he had gone out on the back deck to get some fresh air, Dylan observed what he thought was a deer on all fours until it began to stand up and walk on two feet. He then observed the animal look his way and described it as having a snout looking like a dog, although the face was somewhat gaunt. Dylan is not a small man and is 6 foot 6 inches and he said this creature was much larger. This creature made its way out of the yard and back toward the woods, and he decided to go back in the house and lock the doors. Dylan indicated that this creature scared him to the bone. Both of these small communities are located very close to the Land Between the Lakes area.

Tim's campsite inside North Stewart Forest Area
Stewart County Tennessee

Inside of Tim's comfortable tent, complete with food, stove and cooking utensils.

Chapter 13

Evidence of Removed Campsites

There are certain areas in the LBL which have traces of nice campsites which no longer exist. This fact is supported by telephone poles which had been cut to the ground and in certain places paved areas with what appears to have had bathrooms and shower facilities. In many cases there appears to have been some landscaping done with possibly a bulldozer or excavator, and there is more than one site within the LBL that has been removed. Some of these campsites appear to have been well built with very nice facilities and a question that comes to mind is why not just close these facilities rather than remove them? During the early stages of the LBL's existence, great resources were put into these campgrounds to ensure that they were comfortable and had all the amenities that campers would appreciate. While there are still some nice facilities, particularly in the lower half of the LBL, it would seem peculiar that certain areas are no longer being used that had nice, paved roads and cul-de-sacs with camper slots all around. It is hard to believe that budgetary concerns would shut down the campgrounds in this beautiful park. The following pages include photographs which appear to show these removed campsites. There were many residents on the Land Between the Lakes before the area was converted into this national recreation area and as such there are remains of old home places with porches and other structures still visible. These pictures seem to indicate structures that are not associated with these older home places, but more so with camping facilities although in some cases these pictures may include older structures from that early time period.

One of several block and concrete holding tanks inside the campground. (Photo by Dewey Edwards)

One of several concrete slabs can be found inside the campground. (Photo by Dewey Edwards)

Old drain tile. Part of the campsite drainage system.
(Photo by Dewey Edwards)

These claw marks were found on a tree near a tent
that had the door ripped off in the Upper peninsula
by Hellbent Holler researchers.

These claw marks were found on a tree near a tent
that had the door ripped off in the Upper peninsula
by Hellbent Holler researchers.

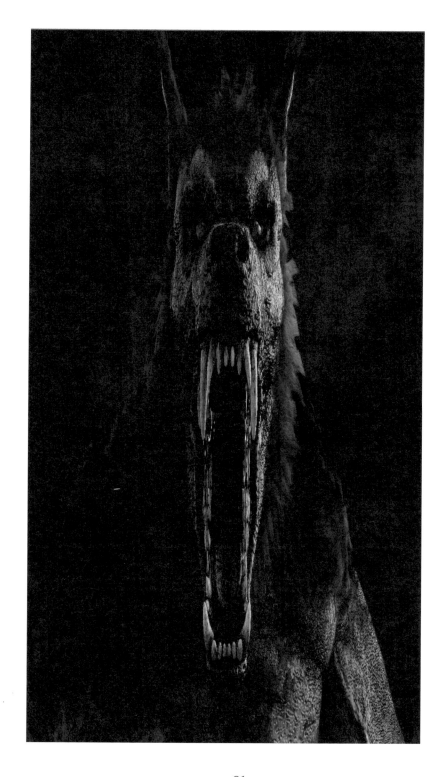

Unusual Padded Footprint with apparent claws.
(Photo by Dewey Edwards)

Human

Dogman

10 FEET

8 FEET

6 FEET

Unusual footprints taken inside the LBL appear to
contain claws. (Photo by Dewey Edwards)

Possible Dogman Origins

Many cryptic researchers and others have speculated about the origins of the Dogman. There are some people that believe these creatures may have been genetically engineered by a government, perhaps even our own government. I think this is probably one theory that could be quickly dismissed as it seems these creatures have been around for some time. There have been to be too many credible witnesses who have reported sightings of these creatures much earlier than our knowledge of genetics would have evolved. It was not until 1985 that DNA testing began, which then brought our knowledge of genetics to a whole new level of understanding. Some witnesses claim that the Dogman creature was used during the Vietnam era war by our government to infiltrate and attack certain enemy positions. I believe this may have been possible due to the apparent intelligence of this creature and if you wanted a near-perfect creature for military purposes it would be hard to find a better candidate. One can only imagine the shock factor of not only having to deal with enemy forces but then having this creature plunged on top of your positions. One theory that I have heard from some researchers, which may be more plausible, is that these creatures were genetically engineered by an alien race many thousands of years ago. If aliens with advanced technology visited our earth in the past it would certainly seem possible that they could have combined the DNA of certain primates with the DNA of the canine ancestors of that time period. It may also be possible that this creature evolved from other animals that are simply not cataloged in our fossil records. Throughout history there have been many references to the possible existence of the Dogman, and this could serve as further evidence of the lineage of this creature. Christopher Columbus reported during his first expeditions of the Caribbean or " New World", that Taino Inhabitants of what is now known as the Bahama Islands, knew of the existence of what was referred to as the Dog headed man. There is some debate as to whether this tribe did exist, and the indigenous people that inhabited these islands in the Caribbean did not refer to themselves by this name. The records of this time period are very sparse, however the fact that these creatures have been spoken of in the past may be evidence enough for their existence. Cynocephaly is the term that is used to refer to a creature that has the head of a dog and body of a man, in mythology.

Chapter 14

Author's Thoughts

As mentioned earlier in this book it is up to the individual reader to conclude whether the incidents that occurred in the upper peninsula are real or myth. When I first heard this story back in1998 I was skeptical of these events although they lighted my interest in the area and the subject matter. My personal belief is that there are simply too many credible witnesses to ignore and in recent years even more witnesses have come forward, many of these witnesses are retired law officers. I think it is very possible that there is a dangerous predator in certain areas of the LBL and I do not believe in what some psychiatrists attempt to push as "mass hysteria", I think this is pseudo-science. I also believe that if there is a dangerous predator in the LBL, that this should not prevent people from enjoying this area. I do believe that we should always be conscious of our surroundings, and you are probably safer in the LBL than you are in Chicago Illinois. As public officials say, always be aware of your surroundings and you should never forget that you are just another animal in the wilderness, and even when armed, you may not be the apex predator in the woods. I have had the privilege of talking with many fine researchers in the cryptozoology field during the course of writing this book. These researchers are meticulous in their research and checking, and then rechecking their facts regarding any investigation. The vast majority of researchers in this field want nothing more than to find out the truth regarding these undocumented species. Many of these researchers use their own money and time to pursue their interest in this field and wish nothing more than to find conclusive evidence of the existence of these cryptic animals. The mountain gorilla was considered a myth and many people concluded that this animal simply did not exist until positive scientific proof was found. It is my hope that more scientists and cryptozoologists will become interested in the LBL area and use new technology such as E- DNA to finally solve the mystery of this creature. The recent budget cuts of Sheriff departments including the LBL area means that the Sheriff's in the upper peninsula and lower peninsula will not be able to offer mutual aid to the authorities in this area. Their argument is sound and reinforced by the fact that if they send officers into this area, they have no radio communication in most of this area. Although discussions are ongoing regarding this mutual aid assistance it is not certain that any agreement can be reached. The net effect of less law enforcement in these areas of the LBL simply means that this area becomes more desolate, isolated and possibly even more dangerous.

Chapter 15

New Evidence and Stories

The author recently interviewed a gentleman that is one of the most credible witnesses that I have spoken with. John is a trapper and has been since he was nine years old. John's father taught him how to trap and hunt when he was a young boy. This very experienced trapper has hunted and trapped just about any varmint you can imagine, all the way from squirrels to grizzly bears. This gentleman also helps with ridding nuisance animals that may be causing harm to someone or a business. This is exactly how I came to meet John, while he was visiting a local marina that I visit and assist on occasions. John was in the process of trapping raccoons that had become a problem at this marina, when I walked by and said hello, John replied "Hello, I've read you book". John had recognized me from the rear of my book cover. I stopped and spoke with John for about fifteen minutes and ask how he liked my book, and we had a pleasant conversation. John then proceeded to tell me of two separate incidents that he had experienced in the LBL.

The first incident he recounted had only happened less than a year before and was in the middle of squirrel season in 2022. John was squirrel hunting in the LBL, near the Lake

Barkley side not too far from this marina, when he came across a set of footprints that he could not identify, please keep in mind that John is a very experienced trapper and hunter that has spent a good portion of his life in the Land Between the Lakes, and other nearby areas. This experienced trapper had left his I-Phone at home, because as is the case in many areas of the LBL, this phone would not work there due to lack of signal. The track that John described was about 9 inches in length and had the pad impressions of a dog. Extending from these pads in front were 5 very large claw impressions. John was able to see more tracks that were left by this creature and followed it for a short while. John said these tracks were made by no animal that he knows, but they are obviously canine, and he knows of no known canine big enough to leave tracks like that. He stated that he did not want to run in to the animal that made these tracks, armed with squirrel loads. He also stated that the depth of these tracks put this animal at over three hundred pounds. He came to this same area the next day with his phone to get a picture, and with proper rounds should he run into the creature that left these tracks, but the heavy rain from the night before had diminished these tracks considerably.

The second account that John related to me was further north on the Kentucky lake section of the LBL, where he was launching a boat to go fishing, He had pulled into a remote boat ramp located not too far from the original massacre site of 1982, when he got out of his truck to launch his boat. When he left the truck, he had a feeling of dread and imminent danger come over him almost immediately. John said I cannot describe what I felt, but my senses were telling me that I was in grave danger. John also observed that there were no animal sounds, and the area was eerily silent. This was early in the morning and there were "No tree frogs, no crickets, Nothing". This is the classic sign as discussed earlier in this book, that many witnesses have observed with these creatures. John wasted no time getting his boat into the water and on his way away from the shore. Even though he had not observed anything in site of this ramp, he could not shake this feeling of being observed and possibly even stalked. According to John, this event occurred around 2017.

Chris is a very credible witness, and a former US Army Lieutenant that I recently interviewed. This is a very recent event that occurred in February of 2024. Chris is a very sharp individual who's extensive military training allows him to be very attentive to detail. Chris and his wife were traveling from Clarksville, Tennessee to Dover Tennessee one night, when they had just passed the bi-county landfill, which services these two towns. This area is in close proximity to the Big Rock area and very near the LBL. Chris noticed something in his peripheral vision and began braking, and at that time a Dogman crossed in front of him, within 15 feet of his minivan. He was able to get a very good look at this creature, with his headlights on high beam. This Dogman had a large coyote in his mouth and ran directly in front of his vehicle. Chris describes this Dogman as running on all fours and being about even in height with the hood of his minivan. This animal was huge, and he estimates the animal weighed at least 350 lbs. Chris describes seeing a human like torso on this animal with human arms and hands. This animal had what he called a boar like fur around its torso, that was dark black. This animal was steering itself with these humanlike arms, and he described the rear of the animal as having more dog-like legs as it was running.

He described the stride of this animal as being like that of a buffalo. The height of the hood of the minivan that Chris owns is about 4 foot and this creature was even with this. Chris estimates the height of the creature would be about 7 feet or over if it stood.

Chris camps in the LBL and he and his wife are avid outdoor people. After seeing this creature up close, they were chilled to the bone, and both of them are having second thoughts about ever camping in the woods again. Chris had heard of the Dogman and was skeptical, but after this sighting, he no longer doubts their existence.

The author was recently in the area not too far from what is known as the Buffalo Pens, when I noticed a new cell phone tower installation. This was a new construction, because equipment was still on site, and the tower had radio repeater antennas located on this tower, with empty helix transmission reels located nearby. This new addition will be of great use to this area and help fill in the many dead signal cell areas as well as assist law enforcement.

Chapter 16

Story of An Aggressive Bigfoot

The author recently made a trip to another residence of an area that is located next to the LBL, to interview another witness, three other researchers were with me on this interview and the gentlemen that we interviewed was deemed to be a credible person, by all the members of this team.

This witness has a nice home on a bay next to the Land between the Lakes. The south side of the bay is owned by private residents of the area, and the north end is where the LBL begins. The first observation that this gentleman made was from the nice, screened deck, or as we call it in the south, a screened-in porch, of his residence facing the bay. This gentleman had heard a very large splash one evening after dusk, and then heard what sounded like bipedal footsteps in the bay near his house. He quickly grabbed his flashlight and a pair of binoculars that he had on his deck and observed a large hairy creature plodding through the water on the other side of the bay. This creature was observed for about thirty seconds before making its way up the bank and back into the tree cover inside the LBL.

Not too many months after this Bigfoot was sighted, this gentleman was on his deck again when he heard the reports from automatic weapons and three round bursts from other weapons. These reports were obviously from military weapons, specifically the M-4, which is the standard issue weapon of the U.S Military. He heard one rifle that was firing on automatic, and then would hear the second rifle that was firing three round bursts, but these rifle bursts were moving as if to drive something in a specific direction. The direction of these rifles shifted from northwest to a true north direction. After a short period of time, he heard the report of a much larger weapon, and this was a single report, after this gunshot, he heard no further weapon's reports.

At some point later this gentleman spoke with a friend that worked at a nearby army base and he indicated that he heard rumors that an aggressive bigfoot in an area of the LBL had been killed and removed by helicopter. This was probably the Chinook helicopter used by the airborne forces at the nearby Fort Campbell Army base.

Brian is another credible witness that the author interviewed recently. Brain is a former Tennessee State Trooper and very credible witness and trained observer. Law enforcement officers are among the most credible witnesses that any investigator will have the privilege to interview. Brian owns a fair amount of land with cattle stock that he takes care of. Brian heard a disturbance near the herd and was able to retrieve is quality night vision scope, as this was later in the evening well beyond dusk. This night vision scope is high quality and military grade and what he observed was a creature that was walking along the edge of the woods that was not human. Brian indicated that this creature walked with a peculiar gait, and had a heat signature that was blue, indicating a very cold signature that was cooler than its surroundings. He observed this creature for a minute or so before it returned to the cover of the trees. Brian has no explanation of what this creature was, but was certain that it was not human, from its strange gait, and large size. Brian also showed me a great picture of a red wolf that he had taken recently on his land. Red wolves are a new species to the area of the LBL, and since his land is very near Lake Barkley, it is obvious that these wolves now reside in the area.

John is yet another credible witness that I spoke with recently. John is an army veteran and former police officer that enjoys hunting in the LBL. John confirmed to me that on a recent hunting trip near the Dover TN entrance of the "Trace", he encountered a black panther. Park officials will tell you that these big cats are not in the LBL area, but as with many other statements that are made by these officials, they are simply wrong.

Chapter 17

Kill Teams

A lot has changed since 1982, and it has been reported that there are teams of former military, or other trained units that form what is known as "Kill Teams". If an aggressive Dogman, or Bigfoot has killed someone or is causing problems, these teams are called in. Unlike the story of the original massacre which involved many confused coroners, and other individuals trying to put together what has happened, and what caused it, the response is much more coordinated. Some witnesses have reported that these individuals may even show up in civilian clothing, with little to no insignia that would identify their purpose. What these teams do show up with is military grade weapons, and equipment to take care of a problem that might involve a large creature or creatures. Reports of these teams suddenly showing up at "incidents", would seem to qualify two things. The first being that the government is well aware that these creatures exist and has a plan for taking care of them. The second being that the government has apparently learned a lot over the past forty years and knows what is out there and lives within areas, such as the LBL.

Strange tracks with claws found in the mud at
Demumbers Bay.
(Photo by Dewey Edwards)

These deer bones were found hanging on tree limbs
near the massacre site.
(Photo by Dewey Edwards)

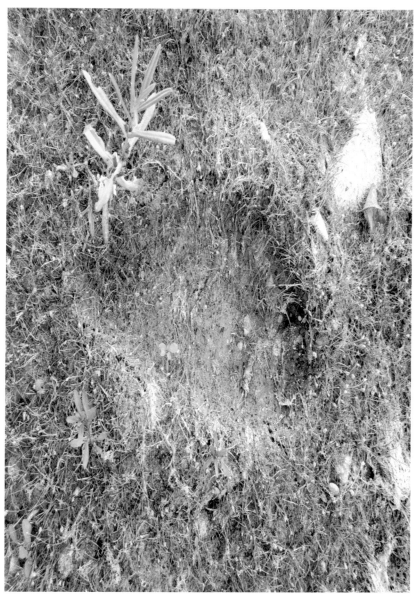

Strange footprint found in the mud at Demumbers Bay.
(Photo by Dewey Edwards)

Strange footprint found in the mud at Demumbers Bay.
(Photo by Dewey Edwards)

Suggested Reading and Videos

Season of the Critters, by Dewey Edwards.

Dewey's books are available on Amazon, or directly from his Facebook page <u>Soggy Bottom Bookstore</u>. Also available on Kindle.

Beasts Between The Rivers, by Martin Groves.

A Trace of Death, by Martin Groves.

Martin's books may be obtained on Amazon, and also by Kindle download.

Elijah Henderson of Cryptid Studies Institute's YouTube video "IF YOU HEAR THIS, RUN!

INHUMANOIDS with Barton Nunnelly, LBL Massacre- Jan Thompson's own words, (You-Tube Video)

Acknowledgments

Many thanks to Dewey Edwards. It would not have been possible to complete this book without his gracious help.

Thanks to Martin Groves who encouraged me to continue writing this book and his experience and knowledge regarding the subject.

Thanks to Jessi and Joe Doyle of Hellbent Holler for their contributions. Great field researchers.

Thanks to the Cryptic Studies Institute, for their advice and research, and Roger's account.

Thanks to Eliza Causey for images contributed for this book.

Thanks to Cryptids and Critters Paranormal group.

Thanks to Dewey Edwards for editing this book and providing some of the photos used.

Made in the USA
Columbia, SC
07 December 2024

48690245R00064